Animal
Groups

Nico

by Carol Levine

PEARSON
Scott
Foresman

DK

Introduction

There are many kinds of animals. Animals belong to different groups. Different animals have different body parts. The parts an animal has can tell us which group it is in.

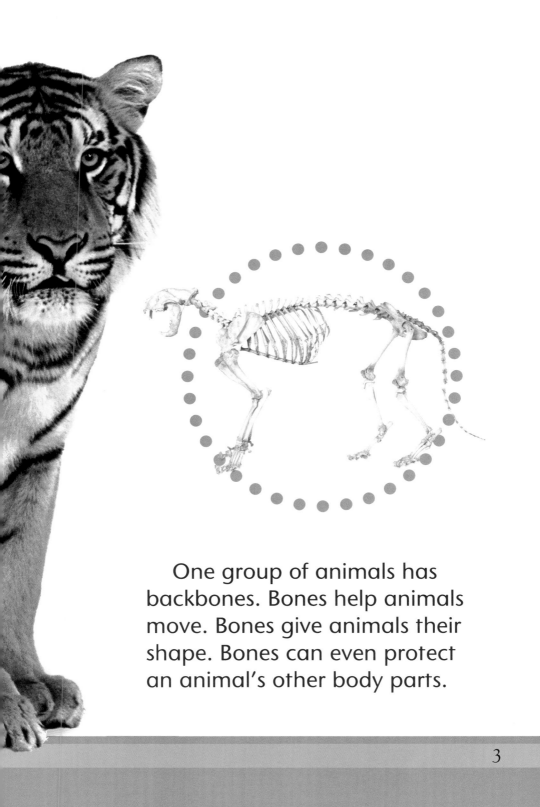

One group of animals has backbones. Bones help animals move. Bones give animals their shape. Bones can even protect an animal's other body parts.

Animals with Backbones

There are many groups of animals with backbones. **Mammals, birds, fish, reptiles,** and **amphibians** are all groups of animals with backbones.

Even though these animals have backbones, they are different from one another. Animals have adapted to their environment.

Mammals

Some animals are mammals. Mammals have backbones. Most mammals have fur or hair on their bodies. Mammals live in many different environments. Mammals are adapted to live in their environment.

Some mammals change colors to hide in their environment. This is called **camouflage.** One mammal that uses camouflage is the arctic fox. In winter the fox's fur changes from gray or brown to white. This helps the fox hide in the snow.

Birds

Some animals are birds. Birds have backbones. They have feathers and wings. Many birds use their feathers and wings to fly.

Birds also live in many different environments. Birds are adapted to live in their environment.

This woodpecker's beak is strong. The beak helps the bird to make holes in trees. The woodpecker's tongue is long and sticky. It uses its tongue to get insects from inside the tree.

shark

Fish

Some animals are fish. Fish have backbones. Fish live in the water. Fish are adapted to live in this environment.

Most fish have scales. Most fish have fins. Scales and fins help fish swim. Fish have **gills.** Gills help fish get the oxygen they need to live.

remora

The remora fish has a sucker on its head. This fish stays safe by using its sucker to stick to other sea animals. Sometimes remoras stick to sharks. Sharks keep remoras safe.

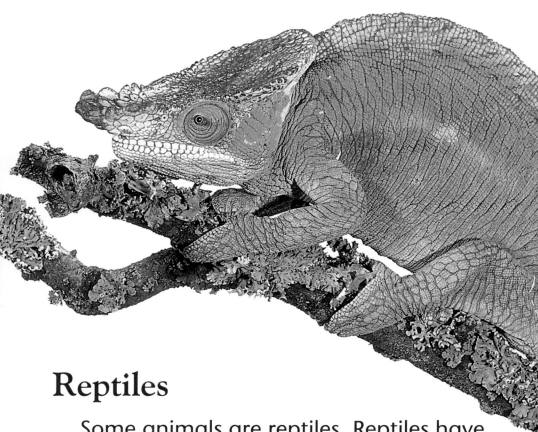

Reptiles

Some animals are reptiles. Reptiles have backbones. They have scales on their skin. These scales protect the animal. Reptiles get cold when the air is cold. They get warm when the air is warm. Some warm reptiles can move fast!

Some reptiles can change colors. Camouflage lets them hide in the places where they live.

The chameleon can change from yellow to green to brown. Different things cause its skin color to change. Sometimes the color changes because the animal is afraid. Camouflage helps the chameleon stay safe.

Amphibians

Some animals are amphibians. Amphibians have backbones. Amphibians live in many different environments. They can live on land and in the water. They are adapted to live in their environment.

This poison dart frog eats insects and turns them into poison. The poison travels through the frog's body and onto its skin. The poison keeps other animals from eating the frog. This way, the frog stays safe.

Animals Without Backbones

There are many animals in the world that do not have backbones. Animals without backbones live in many different environments. They are adapted to their environment.

Animals without backbones need to protect their body parts too. Snails have soft bodies. Their hard shells help them stay safe. Jellyfish also have soft bodies. But they can sting animals that want to harm them.

Insects

Insects have three main body parts and six legs. Many insects have antennae on their heads. These antennae help the insects feel, smell, hear, and taste things.

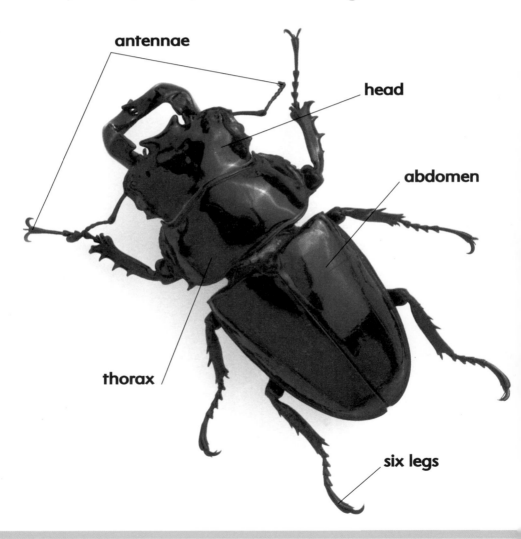

antennae

head

abdomen

thorax

six legs

Like all insects, the cicada (suh KAY duh) does not have bones. The cicada can sing. The loud singing of some cicadas keeps them safe. Birds do not like this sound. They stay away from the cicadas.

Worms

There are lots of different kinds of worms. Worms do not have backbones. Earthworms' bodies have more than one hundred parts.

Earthworms live in the soil. Damp soil
helps keep the skin of the worms wet.
They must stay damp to be able to get air.

Octopuses

Octopuses are sea animals without backbones. They can make clouds of ink to stay safe. Ink makes it hard for other animals to find octopuses. Octopuses can also use camouflage to hide.

Animals with backbones live in many places in the world. Animals without backbones do too. Wherever an animal lives, it is adapted to its environment.

Glossary

amphibian an animal with a backbone and smooth, wet skin that lives on land and in water

bird an animal with a backbone, feathers, and wings that hatches from an egg

camouflage a color or shape that makes an animal hard to see

fish an animal with a backbone, scales, and fins that lives in water

gills body parts that help fish get oxygen from water

insect an animal with three body parts and six legs that does not have a backbone

mammal an animal with a backbone and hair or fur

reptile an animal with a backbone and scales that hatches from an egg

What did you learn?

1. How does an arctic fox's fur change in the winter?

2. How does camouflage protect a chameleon?

3. **Writing** in Science Snails and jellyfish do not have backbones. Write to explain how these animals stay safe. Include details from the book to support your answer.

4. 🎯 **Alike and Different** How is an octopus like an earthworm? How is it different?

Science

Genre	Comprehension Skill	Text Features	Science Content
Nonfiction	Alike and Different	• Call Outs • Glossary	

$1.49
859984
t99-
215-P

NO Exchange
Media
Books

Scott Foresman Science 2.2

scottforesman.com

ISBN 0-328-13773-1

90000

9 780328 137732

Quick Trip

By Jennifer Franklin
Illustrated by Erin Eitter Kono

Editorial Offices: Glenview, Illinois • Parsippany, New Jersey • New York, New York
Sales Offices: Boston, Massachusetts • Duluth, Georgia • Glenview, Illinois
Coppell, Texas • Sacramento, California • Mesa, Arizona

ISBN: 0-328-21398-5

    8 9 10 V008 12 11 10 09
CC1